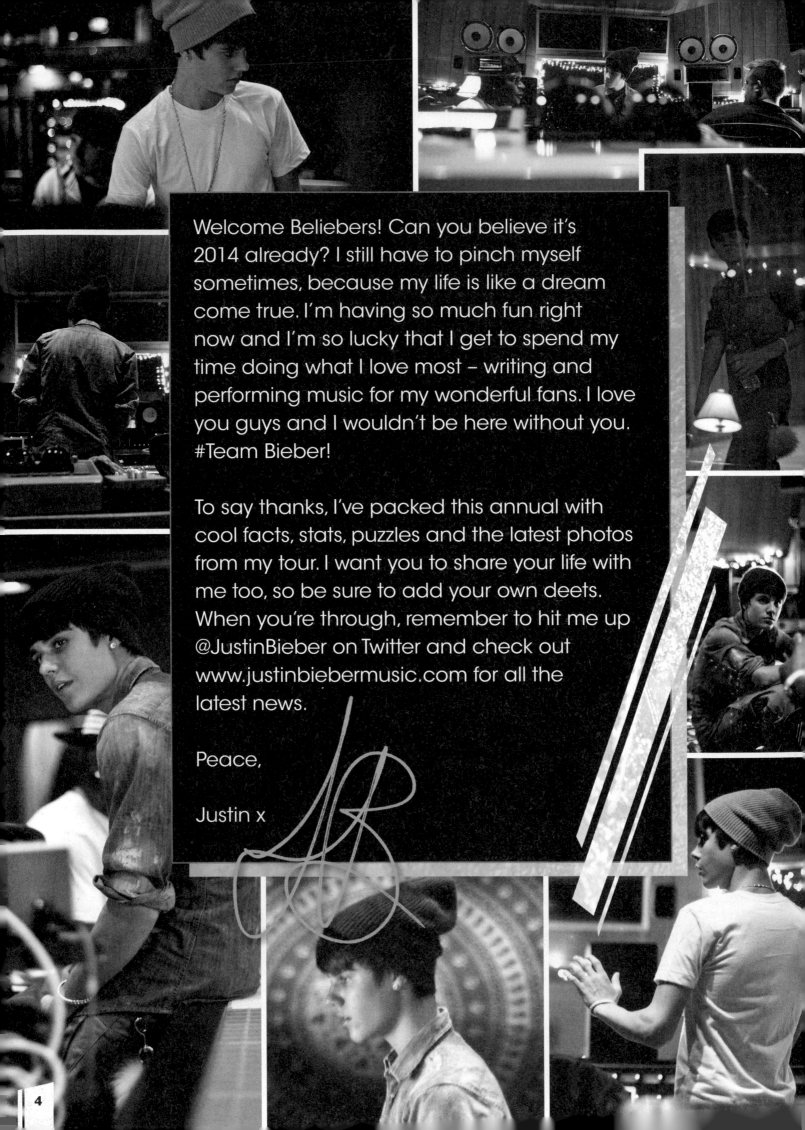

Welcome Beliebers! Can you believe it's 2014 already? I still have to pinch myself sometimes, because my life is like a dream come true. I'm having so much fun right now and I'm so lucky that I get to spend my time doing what I love most – writing and performing music for my wonderful fans. I love you guys and I wouldn't be here without you. #Team Bieber!

To say thanks, I've packed this annual with cool facts, stats, puzzles and the latest photos from my tour. I want you to share your life with me too, so be sure to add your own deets. When you're through, remember to hit me up @JustinBieber on Twitter and check out www.justinbiebermusic.com for all the latest news.

Peace,

Justin x

CONTENTS

THE BIEBER BUZZ

Fact File

Name:	**Justin Drew Bieber**
Nationality:	**Canadian**
D.O.B:	**1st March 1994**
Star Sign:	**Pisces**
Birthplace:	**London, Ontario, Canada**
Lives:	**Calabasas, LA and Atlanta, Georgia, USA**
Nicknames:	**JB, JBiebz, Biebz or Kid Rauhl**
Hair:	**Brown**
Eyes:	**Brown**
BFFs:	**Ryan Butler & Chaz Summers**
Significant Others:	**Pattie Mallette (Mum), Jeremy Bieber (Dad), Jazmyn Bieber (Sister), Jaxon Bieber (Brother)**
Instruments Played:	**Drums, guitar, piano and trumpet**

JB loves ...
- Beliebers
- Basketball
- Ice hockey
- Italian food

JB is sooo over...
- Ugg Boots on girls
- Being labelled a 'teen heartthrob'

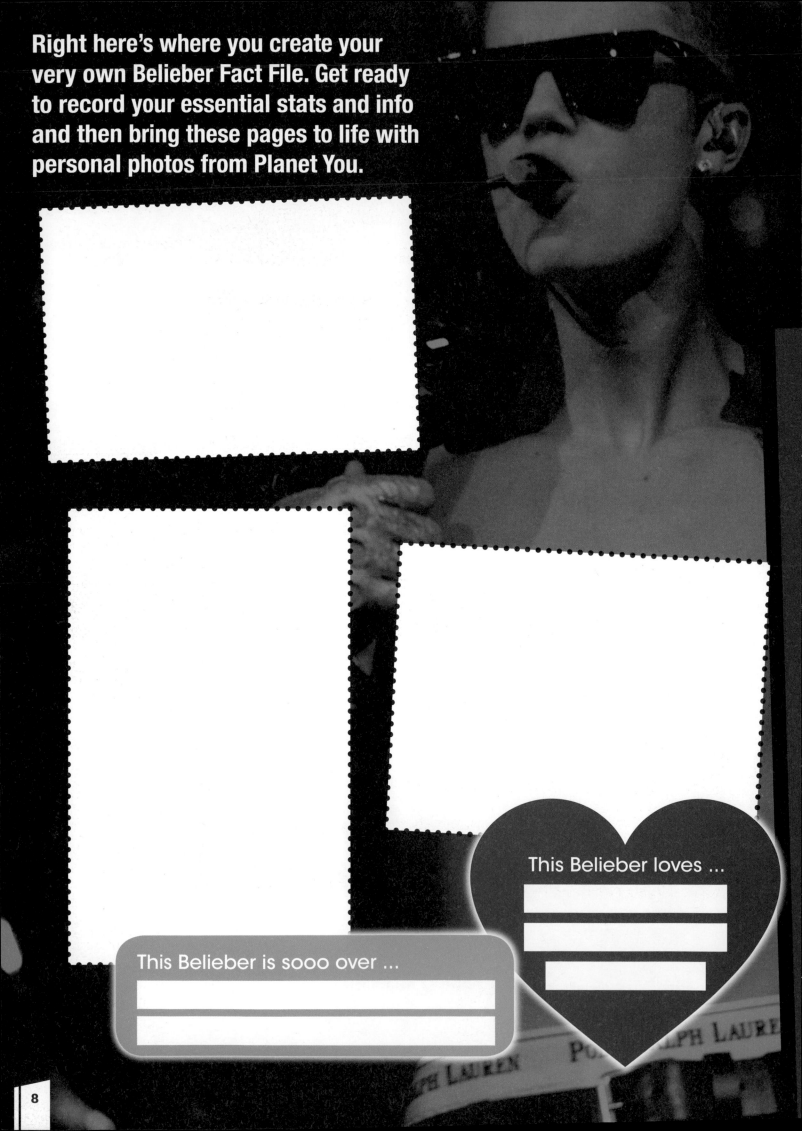

Right here's where you create your very own Belieber Fact File. Get ready to record your essential stats and info and then bring these pages to life with personal photos from Planet You.

This Belieber loves ...

This Belieber is sooo over ...

Fact File

Name:

Nationality:

D.O.B:

Star Sign:

Birthplace:

Lives:

Nicknames:

Hair:

Eyes:

BFFs:

Significant Others:

Instruments Played:

JUSTIN'S STORY I:

IN THE BEGINNING ...

On March 1st 1994 in London, Ontario, Canada, Pattie Mallette and Jeremy Bieber welcomed their child into the world.

Thousands of babies are born every day, so what made this one so special? How did a Canadian boy-next-door become one of the most famous faces in the world, able to sell out the globe's biggest arenas in minutes? For Justin Drew Bieber, it was never about the destination, his journey was what really mattered.

These days, JB is a global icon, admired as much for his film-star looks and fashion sense as for his incredible stage shows, but first and foremost, Justin is a musician. From an early age he displayed a precocious talent for music. He could turn his hand to many instruments (though, at the time, most were twice his size) and could sing with the kind of control and power most professional singers would kill for.

For all his technical ability however, it was Justin's ability to connect with people that really set him apart This rare gift and the lessons Justin learnt growing up set him on the path he walks today.

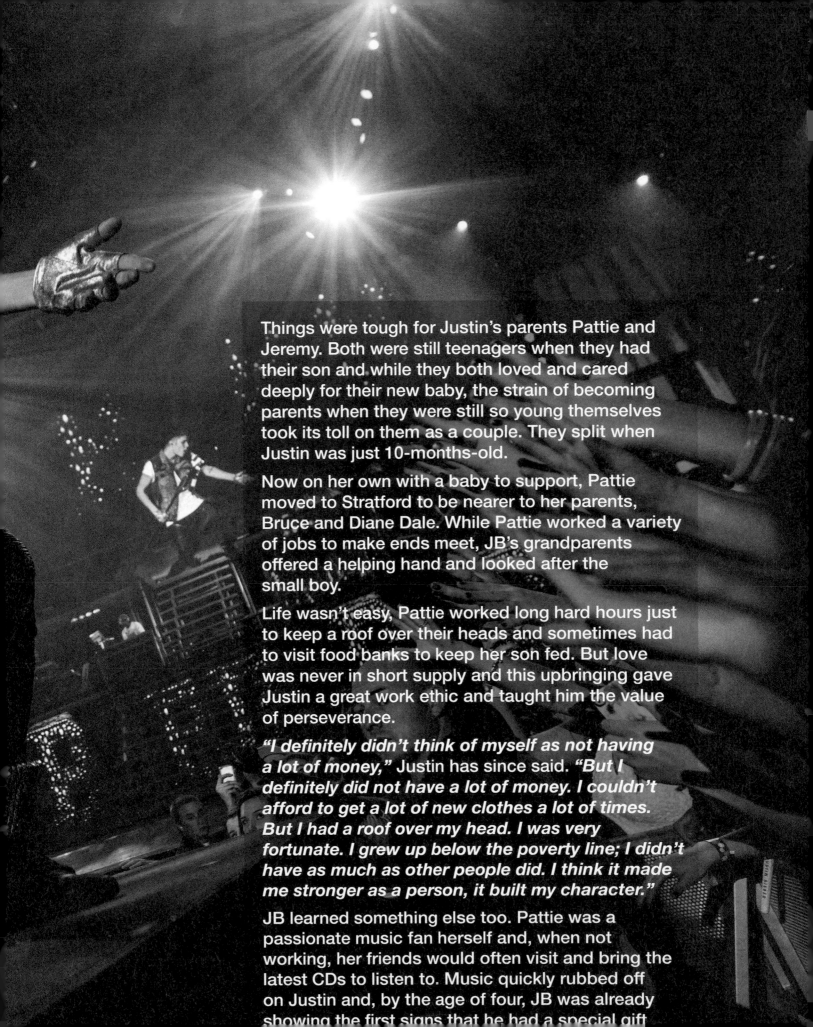

Things were tough for Justin's parents Pattie and Jeremy. Both were still teenagers when they had their son and while they both loved and cared deeply for their new baby, the strain of becoming parents when they were still so young themselves took its toll on them as a couple. They split when Justin was just 10-months-old.

Now on her own with a baby to support, Pattie moved to Stratford to be nearer to her parents, Bruce and Diane Dale. While Pattie worked a variety of jobs to make ends meet, JB's grandparents offered a helping hand and looked after the small boy.

Life wasn't easy, Pattie worked long hard hours just to keep a roof over their heads and sometimes had to visit food banks to keep her son fed. But love was never in short supply and this upbringing gave Justin a great work ethic and taught him the value of perseverance.

"I definitely didn't think of myself as not having a lot of money," Justin has since said. *"But I definitely did not have a lot of money. I couldn't afford to get a lot of new clothes a lot of times. But I had a roof over my head. I was very fortunate. I grew up below the poverty line; I didn't have as much as other people did. I think it made me stronger as a person, it built my character."*

JB learned something else too. Pattie was a passionate music fan herself and, when not working, her friends would often visit and bring the latest CDs to listen to. Music quickly rubbed off on Justin and, by the age of four, JB was already showing the first signs that he had a special gift

ALBUMS & EPs

TITLE	RELEASE DATE
My World	November 2009
My World 2.0	March 2010
My Worlds: The Collection	November 2010
My Worlds Acoustic	November 2010
Never Say Never: The Remixes	February 2011
Under the Mistletoe	November 2011
Believe	June 2012
Believe Acoustic	January 2013

Biebz also has 'featured artist' credits on five singles including Next to You with Chris Brown and #ThatPower with Will.i.am.

DISCOGRAPHY

Call yourself a Belieber? If you don't already own JB's complete discography, then get downloading.

SINGLES

TITLE	RELEASE DATE
One Time	2009
One Less Lonely Girl	2009
Baby feat. Ludacris	2010
Eenie Meenie feat. Sean Kingston	2010
Somebody to Love	2010
U Smile	2010
Pray	2010
Never Say Never feat. Jaden Smith	2011
Mistletoe	2011
Boyfriend	2012
Turn to You	2012
As Long as You Love Me feat. Big Sean	2012
Beauty and a Beat feat. Nicki Minaj	2012
Right Here feat. Drake	2013
All Around the World feat. Ludacris	2013

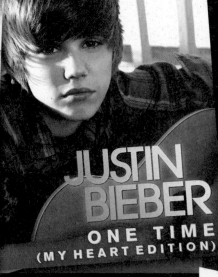

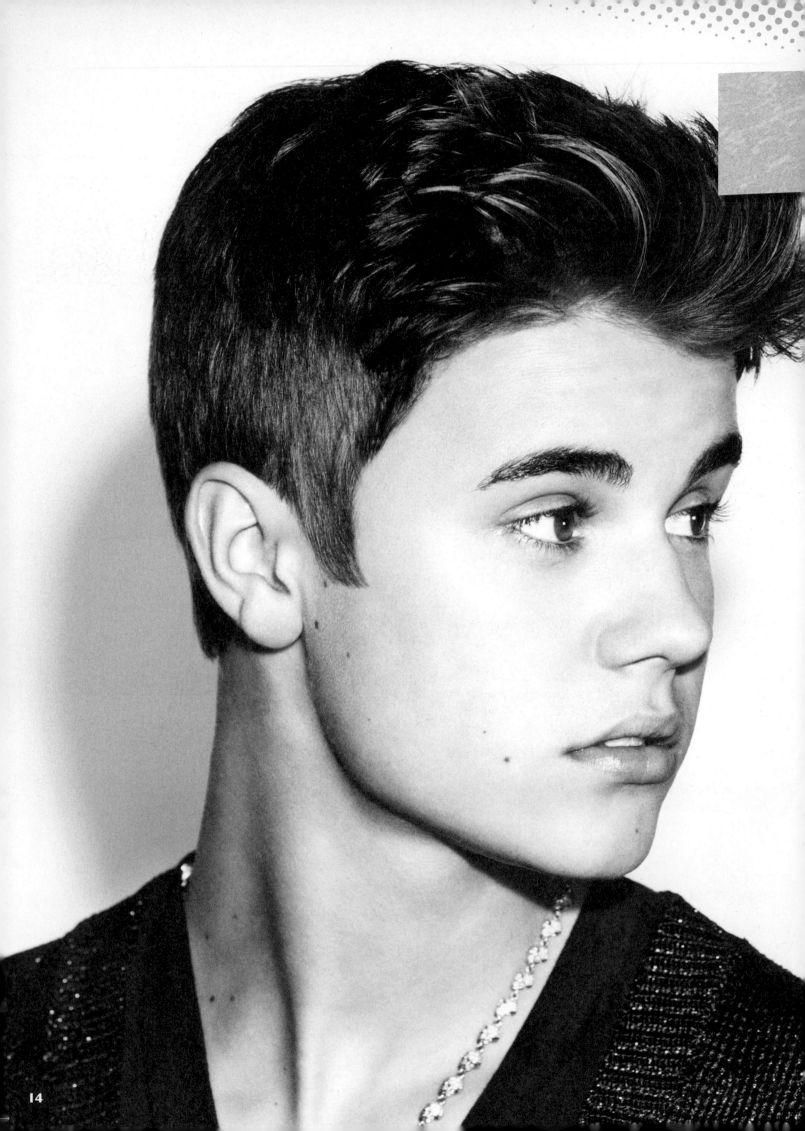

BELIEVE

HOW WAS JUSTIN GOING TO FOLLOW HIS FIRST TWO ULTRA-SUCCESSFUL ALBUMS? ALL HE HAD TO DO WAS COMPLETELY OVERHAUL HIS SOUND AND RELEASE A HIT-PACKED RECORD WITH A NEW MATURE STYLE. FORTUNATELY, JB HAD 'BELIEVE' UP HIS SLEEVE. HERE'S THE STORY BEHIND THE SMASH ALBUM'S GREATEST HITS...

BOYFRIEND

For most, this was their first taste of the brand new JB – breathy rapping combined to maximum effect with Justin's strong falsetto. Justin hooked up with singer/producer Mike Posner, who hit the tops of the charts himself with the song 'Cooler Than Me' to to create an instant classic.

"With Justin, we kept the studio pretty locked down just because he can go from zero to insane in a matter of five minutes!" Mike revealed. *"It was definitely insane. I was just honoured to be a part of the project."*

DIE IN YOUR ARMS

Not one to shy away from a challenge, JB worked with super-producer Rodney Jerkins, a.k.a. Dark Child, on this track, a slick R&B song about love and meeting the girl of your dreams. Rodney has twiddled the studio knobs on some of the biggest songs in history by artists including Beyoncé, Lady Gaga and Michael Jackson, but was clearly impressed with Biebz.

"There were plenty of moments when he would nail the notes and I would be like, 'Wow'," he explained. *"To me, he is this generation's new great."*

ALL AROUND THE WORLD

In case anyone was in any doubt that Justin had matured between albums, one listen to this track had them up to speed! An electronic, club-tastic, dancefloor-filler, it was the first time Justin had teamed up with Ludacris since they conquered the charts together on 'Baby'. JB's vocals soared and Luda's rap hit the tone!

"Once again, dynamic duos are back! JB, Luda!" Ludacris rapped. *"I love everything about you. You're imperfectly perfect! Everyone's itching for beauty, but they're just scratching the surface."*

BELIEVE

You don't have to spend long following JB on Twitter to realise his relationship with his fans is one of the most important things in his life. To mark this he wanted to dedicate a track to his Beliebers and 'Believe' didn't disappoint.

"This is a track I wrote for my fans and it's about how they inspired me. Listen to the words ... It means a lot," JB explained. *"I wrote it on my birthday – it was midnight in the studio and Scooter wanted to sing happy birthday to me but I was like 'no, let me finish this song!'"*

RIGHT HERE

Justin proved he has a talent for working with up and coming new producers when he recorded this banger. Hit Boy had worked with Lil' Wayne and Eminem but his name received much wider attention when he worked his magic on JB and Drake's track. Fully loaded with swagger, the track proved such a hit with fans that they started a Twitter campaign to get the two superstars to record a video for the song together!

AS LONG AS YOU LOVE ME

Loaded with bass and boasting a hook that could turn even the most fervent Bieber hater into a full-blown Belieber, 'As Long As You Love Me' saw Justin again teaming up with Dark Child. At a top-secret album preview for journalists and music industry peeps in London JB revealed it to be one of his favourite tracks on the album saying, *"Man, this is a really good song!"* We couldn't agree more.

THE BELIEVE TOUR

SET LIST

All Around the World

Take You

Catching Feelings

Medley: One Time/Eenie Meenie/
Somebody to Love

Love Me Like You Do

She Don't Like the Lights

Die in Your Arms

Right Here

Fairytale

Beautiful (feat. Carly Rae Jepsen)

Out of Town Girl

Be Alright

Fall

Never Let You Go

Never Say Never

Beauty and a Beat

One Less Lonely Girl

As Long As You Love Me

Believe

Encore

Boyfriend

Baby

Paris

Las Veg

Alabama

Zurich

Munich

Los Angeles

California

"Coming down right from the beginning of the show, it's me and the wings for about 30 seconds. It's such a big moment. People are just captivated and there's nothing else going on, so that moment is going to bleed into their memory."

Believe Tour Quick Triv

- Carly Rae Jepson, The Wanted, Cody Simpson and Jaden Smith all performed on the Believe Tour.

- In total, the tour will last just under a year

- Justin will perform 124 dates in all. 79 in America, 41 in Europe, two in Asia and two in Africa.

- Every single seat on every single date on the first American leg of the tour sold out, all 711,729 of them!

- The biggest audience JB performed in front of in one night is 43,817!

- JB's date at Madison Square Garden in New York sold out in 22 seconds!

Philadelphia

IN HIS OWN WOR

So much is written and spoken about JB, but what does the man himself have to say about his career and life as a celebrity? We've rounded up some classic Justin quotes so you can get to know the man behind the music.

On what people think of him ...

"The biggest misconception about me is that I'm a bad person. I get upset about that. I have a big heart. I want to be a good role model, but some people want me to fail."

On how long he can stay famous ...

"I don't think that I'm going to be boiling hot for the rest of my career. I think that, if I'm not on top, it would be because I didn't want to be. It would be a time when I wanted to take a break and do movies or take a break and raise a family."

On his rise to fame ...

"It's been pretty amazing. I'm glad I get to travel the world and I'm just really thankful that I've just been able to do what I love."

On overcoming the dangers of the industry ...

"You know, being in the music business sometimes can be a little shady. There's a lot of people that try to get inside and, you know, try to mess things up. But, you've just got to keep your family close and remain humble and you'll go far."

On being Justin Bieber ...

"I'm just a regular kid. I make good grilled cheese and I like girls."

On how it feels to become famous ...

"My world got very big, very fast, and based on a lot of sad examples from the past, a lot of people expect me to get lost in it."

On his expectations for his music ...

"I want girls to hear my music and want to play it again because it made their hearts feel good."

On proving the naysayers wrong ...

"Haters will say what they want, but their hate will never stop you from chasing your dream."

On his dream life ...

"I want my world to be fun. No parents, no rules, no nothing. Like, no one can stop me. No one can stop me."

On the ladeez ...

"It was like I opened my eyes one day and noticed that the world was full of beautiful girls.

And I've had a hard time thinking about anything else since then."

On his looks ...

"Not trying to be arrogant, but if I walked down the street and a girl saw me, she might take a look back because maybe I'm good-looking, right?"

On his secret talent ...

"Now I'm really glad that I speak French, because, let's face it; girls dig it when a guy speaks French. They call it the language of love, and that ain't no coincidence. Plus, I love my French fans! Très jolie!"

On his grand plan ...

"I'm here for a reason, and I'm here for a lifetime. And no-one is going to get rid of me."

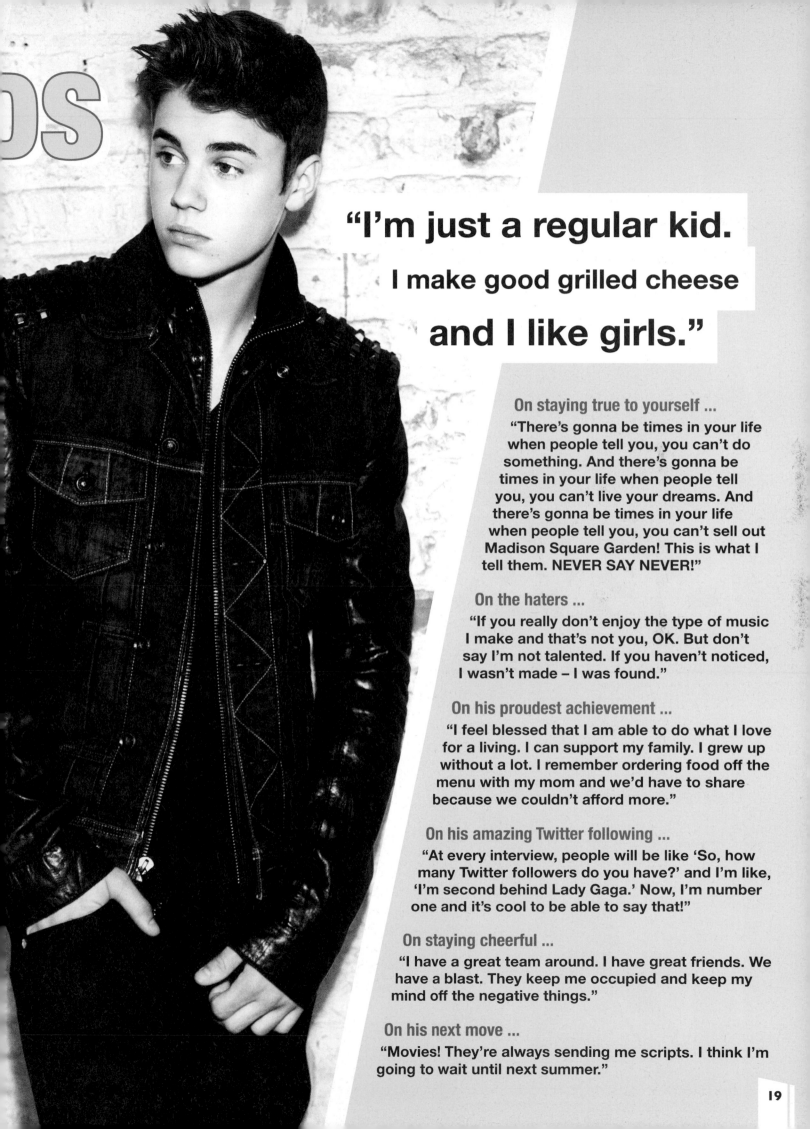

"I'm just a regular kid. I make good grilled cheese and I like girls."

On staying true to yourself ...

"There's gonna be times in your life when people tell you, you can't do something. And there's gonna be times in your life when people tell you, you can't live your dreams. And there's gonna be times in your life when people tell you, you can't sell out Madison Square Garden! This is what I tell them. NEVER SAY NEVER!"

On the haters ...

"If you really don't enjoy the type of music I make and that's not you, OK. But don't say I'm not talented. If you haven't noticed, I wasn't made – I was found."

On his proudest achievement ...

"I feel blessed that I am able to do what I love for a living. I can support my family. I grew up without a lot. I remember ordering food off the menu with my mom and we'd have to share because we couldn't afford more."

On his amazing Twitter following ...

"At every interview, people will be like 'So, how many Twitter followers do you have?' and I'm like, 'I'm second behind Lady Gaga.' Now, I'm number one and it's cool to be able to say that!"

On staying cheerful ...

"I have a great team around. I have great friends. We have a blast. They keep me occupied and keep my mind off the negative things."

On his next move ...

"Movies! They're always sending me scripts. I think I'm going to wait until next summer."

Car Crazy

Justin is making a name for himself as a serious car collector. He's been spotted driving in a host of fancy rides recently including a Porsche Turbo 997, a swanky Ferrari F40, a super-fast Lamborghini Gallardo, a Range Rover (a 16th birthday present from Usher!) and a Cadillac CTS-V that he had 'tricked-out' by West Coast Customs. His best-known ride, however is the chrome Fisker electric car that manager Scooter bought him for his 18th birthday and presented to him during an appearance on Ellen DeGeneres' chat show!

Beyond The Hype

Ice Ice Baby

JB has always been sports crazy! He is a huge ice hockey fan and supports the Toronto Blue Jays. But Justin's no sports channel sofa surfer – whenever he can, he hits the ice himself. He also loves soccer and in 2011, he jumped at the chance to train with Chelsea and Barcelona!

Bieber The Baller

One of Justin's favourite things to do is play basketball. Whenever his schedule allows he likes nothing better than to sit courtside, catch up with celebrity mates and watch a game. He's a pretty good player too as he demonstrated at the 2011 NBA All-Star Celebrity game.

Just's Wander-lust

While he was growing up, Justin didn't travel far outside his home town. After three world tours and countless promo trips, he's more than made up for that! And though these days he might need a disguise to leave his hotels unnoticed, he still finds the time to sneak out and explore new cities.

SK8R BOI

While taking a break from recording 'Believe', Justin tweeted his followers to let them know he was skating at a friend's house. Like most normal guys right? Wrong! The friend in question was rap superstar, and fellow skater, Lil' Wayne!

Home Town Hero

Nothing makes Justin happier than simply catching up with the family and friends that know him best. He may not busk on the steps of the local theatre anymore, but JB's at his happiest hanging with his best buds Ryan and Chaz, where he's free to be just Justin from Stratford.

STAR Quotes

Album sales, Twitter followers and record-breaking tours tell you Justin Bieber really is the real deal. But what do other celebrities think of JB? Are there many famous Beliebers? What do you think!

"I'm amazed by Justin Bieber. I don't know how he handles this crazy level of fame. I mean, it's tough for adults, let alone teens."
Movie star and jazz musician Harry Connick Jr. understands the pressure of fame.

"Justin, bless him, he's a very sweet guy. He had a pair of his purple Bieber glasses in his pocket and he said, 'Oh yeah, give these to Lily-Rose.' She was very chuffed about that. She was very touched. He's a good guy. A sweet guy."
Hollywood icon Johnny Depp revealed JB went out of his way for his daughter Lily-Rose.

"People honestly think I'm kidding about Bieber. My mom is so confused. She's like, 'Evan, really?' I'm like, 'Go see 'Never Say Never'. You'll understand.'"

Evan Rachel Wood once dated Marilyn Manson, no wonder her mum was surprised to find out she was so into JB!

"He's my dude. I'm a Belieber! I got mad Bieber Fever! I'm not afraid to admit it!"

Loud and definitely proud, Jersey Shore star Pauly D is a Bieber fanatic and doesn't care who knows it!

"I'm still trying to grow my hair out like him. It's tough because I have really curly hair so I'm trying to flat-iron it and get that hairdo."

Funny man Will Ferrell admits that Justin is a major source of inspiration.

"Go see 'Never Say Never'. This fever cannot be cured!"

Forgetting Sarah Marshall star and the voice of Gossip Girl, Kristen Bell often tweets about her love for Justin!

"When we first got told it was a boy, my middle son Romeo, he was like, 'How about Justin Bieber as a name?' Justin Bieber Beckham. Now that we know it's a girl, he's like, 'Well, how about Justine?'"

Victoria Beckham revealed that a house full of Beliebers caused problems when she found out she was pregnant again.

"Nobody was rocking like that at 16 years old."

Kanye West knows true talent when he sees it.

"He's really cool; he's got lots of advice. When he visited the UK last month he came to my house. Perrie (from Little Mix) was there, and he spent the night with us. We had a KFC."

One Direction's Zayn Malik admits that he goes to JB for advice.

"I cried twice during Justin Bieber: Never Say Never and I want the world to know that!"

Anthony Kiedis of the Red Hot Chili Peppers is an 'out and proud' Belieber!

"He has this presence like Buddha. He's like the young prince. I went up to him at the MTV Movie Awards to say 'hi' and security was like, 'Whoa, whoa.' He was ready to take me down. Bieber just does this two finger wave, like, he's OK. So he's very cool. Bieber's the bomb."

Transformers star Shia LaBeouf loves JB's cool.

"I have Bieber fever. I spammed him on Twitter about five times and said 'Hey Justin it's Chloe, I play Hit-Girl in Kick-Ass'. I tried to be very nonchalant so he would think 'she's cool, I better Tweet her back!' He didn't though, I'm heartbroken!"

Movie it-girl Chloe Moretz may be tough on screen but she still gets giggly talking about JB.

"I do have Bieber fever. He is the most adorable and sweetest. Oh he's so sweet."

Oscar-winning actress Jennifer Hudson is a long-time JB fan.

Janice Joplin
Metallica
Drake
Beyoncé
Tupac
Lil' Wayne
Lil Twist
Stevie Wonder
Kanye West
Taylor Swift
Frank Ocean
Chris Brown
Boyz II Men
Michael Jackson

On JB's iPod

"Lil Twist is one of my best friends ... He's the one who introduced me to Wayne and Wayne at the studio I'm working at ... We went skating at Wayne's house the other day. He's got the dopest skate ramps on the roof of his house."

"Michael Jackson was able to reach audiences from young to old: he never limited himself."

"Besides Usher, the person I've learned the most from is probably Drake. He's given me good advice ... We just text and stuff but he's a great guy."

"Just being in the studio with Kanye is amazing. He's so creative and he's really smart. He was talking about going out of the box and making it cool. He just wants me to make records that people wouldn't necessarily think I would do."

"My favourite rappers of all time are Tupac, Andre 3000, Eminem, Nas, Lil' Wayne and Jay-Z."

Yeah, _____ _____, Nicki Minaj, Justin,

Show _____ _____, tonight I wanna show _____ _____, (eh, eh, eh),
What you got, a _____ could've never bought (eh, eh, eh).

We gonna _____ like it's 3012 tonight,
I wanna show you all the _____ things in _____,
So just _____ about the world, we're _____ tonight,
I'm coming for ya, I'm coming for ya.

Cause all I _____,
Is a beauty and a beat,
Who can _____ my _____ complete,
It's all about _____,
When the _____ makes you _____,
Baby, do it _____ you do,
Cause...

_____ _____, girl, I can feel your _____ _____ (eh, eh, eh),
Take a _____, you're on the hottest _____ now, oh (eh, eh, eh).

We gonna _____ like it's 3012 tonight,
I wanna _____ you all the _____ things in life,
So just _____ about the world, we're _____ tonight,
I'm coming for ya, I'm coming for ya.

Cause all I _____,
Is a beauty and a beat,
Who can _____ my _____ complete,
It's all about _____,
When the _____ makes you _____,
Baby, do it _____ you do.

In time, _____ lines, b-bitches couldn't get on my incline,
World _____, it's mine, ten little _____, on a big sign,
_____ _____, you know I'mma hit 'em with the ether,
Buns out, wiener, but I gotta keep an eye out for _____,
Beauty, beauty and the beast,
Beauty from the _____, beautiful confessions of the _____,
Beast, beauty from the _____, we don't get deceased,
Every time a beauty on the beats.

(Yeah, yeah, yeah, yeah, let's go, let's go),
Body rock, girl, I wanna feel your body rock.

Cause all... (all I need is love) I need,
Is a beauty and a beat,
Who can make my life complete,
It's all... (all I need is you) about you,
When the music makes you move,
Baby, do it like you do.

MISSING LYRICS:
Beauty AND A Beat

NEW COLLABS

Over the course of his career, JB has had the opportunity to work with with some of the best in the business. Here are a few of his finest musical collaborations

Carly has been joining JB on stage during the 'Believe' Tour. And she's full of respect for Justin's talents. "If there's anybody who I think can pull off what it means to be a professional performer, It's Justin," she revealed.

COLLABORATOR: CARLY RAE JEPSON
TRACK: BEAUTIFUL

COLLABORATOR: USHER
TRACK: THE CHRISTMAS SONG
(Chestnuts Roasting On An Open Fire)

Usher's been with Justin from the beginning and he's a constant source of advice and wisdom. "He has had an incredible few years," Usher explained recently. "But I'm going to continue to push him to be his best self."

COLLABORATOR: LUDACRIS
TRACK: BABY AND ALL AROUND THE WORLD

Luda is someone who's really seen JB grow. After working with him on 'Baby', he was back for the 'Believe' album sessions. "We did the song 'Baby' a long time ago, which made history. We're here to make history again," Luda explained. "He's' growing into the manhood stage and his records are reflecting that."

COLLABORATOR: DRAKE
TRACK: RIGHT HERE

Superstar rapper Drake and JB are mutual fans of each other and great mates. The pair recorded 'Right Here Together' for Justin's album and JB returned the favour by remixing Drake's track 'Trust Issues'. "He's a talented kid," Drake says. "To hear him even remix that song is crazy. That's incredible."

COLLABORATOR: NICKI MINAJ
TRACK: BEAUTY AND A BEAT

Justin and Nicki created a classic when they recorded together. Their sexy video and raunchy live performances even had fans speculating that this might be more than simply a musical collaboration! JB fuelled the gossip recently when posted a pic of Nicki on Instagram and wrote 'No caption needed'.

COLLABORATOR: BIG SEAN
TRACK: AS LONG AS YOU LOVE ME

Superstar US rapper Big Sean and JB hooked up to work on 'As Long As You Love Me' together. You can often catch them chatting on Twitter. When Justin headed out on tour Big Sean sent him a good luck message. '@justinbieber u already know boi! Stay safe! Tell 'em that Detroit player said what up doe when u touch down overseas!'

COLLABORATOR: SEAN KINGSTON
TRACK: EENIE MEENIE

JB and Sean have been friends since they worked together on Eenie Meenie. "I met Justin before he was the teenage phenom that he is now. I don't really have that same chemistry with some celebrities," Sean says of their friendship. "God just made it happen." Recently, Justin rapped a verse on Sean's track 'Won't Stop'. "He's pretty tight," Sean says of Justin's rapping skills. "Nice for someone who doesn't do it that much."

COLLABORATOR: WILL.I.AM
TRACK: #THATPOWER

Will.i.am is full of praise for Justin. At the Teen Choice Awards 2012 he gushed, "I work with Justin, he's nice, very talented, beyond what people probably think he's capable of. Justin's career is going to be a long career, ... Maybe people can't see it now but 10-20 years from now, he'll still be around."

JUSTIN'S STORY II
BECOMING THE BIEBZ

Pattie and her music-loving friends spotted Justin's talent early. As a pre-schooler he was already picking out songs on the drums, guitar and piano.

When he turned five, Pattie enrolled Justin in Stratford's Jeanne Sauve Catholic School in Stratford, a French language school. Justin soon settled in. As well as being music crazy, JB was also mad for sports. He played American footballand also joined the school's ice hockey club. It was a good decision as fellow club members include Chaz Somers and Ryan Butler, who remain Justin's best mates to this day.

When he wasn't kicking back with Ryan and Chaz or playing sport, Justin could be found at home making music. He practised his instruments religiously every day and listened to the radio constantly, picking up tricks from the artists he heard.

Although Justin wasn't living with his dad, Jeremy was still a big part of his life, And just like JB, he was a huge music fan.

"Dad's the one who got me into classic rock and then turned me on to stuff like Guns N' Roses and Metallica," Justin revealed. "I have a great relationship with my dad. When I was younger, he taught me how to play some songs on the guitar, like 'Knockin' on Heaven's Door' by Bob Dylan."

JB was making music purely for the love of it and, with consistent practice, he improved quickly. It wasn't long before his home became too small to accommodate his talent. It was time to take his passion to the next level, at just 12-years-old JB was ready to make his first public performance ...

JEREMY BIEBER

Who can forget the moment in Justin Bieber: Never Say Never when proud dad Jeremy stands on the side of the stage with tears in his eyes and watches Justin perform for thousands of fans? Although Jeremy and Pattie split when JB was very young, the father and son are very close. In fact, the two have matching seagull tattoos inked on their hips.

"My life is my son. He is the most talented person I know and he's a 'looker' too (just like his dad)!"

Family Guy

DESPITE HIS FAME AND FORTUNE, AT HEART JUSTIN IS STILL THE SAME YOUNG LAD FROM STRATFORD. FAMILY WAS VITAL TO HIM GROWING UP AND TO THIS DAY, IS STILL HIS NUMBER ONE PRIORITY. MEET THE MOST IMPORTANT PEOPLE IN JB'S LIFE.

Honorary family members

SCOOTER BRAUN

So much more than a manager, Scooter has become like a protective big brother to Justin since he discovered him in 2008. Justin's mum Pattie spent hours grilling Braun before agreeing to let him manage JB back in the day and Scooter's never let Justin – or Pattie – down!

USHER

The first celebrity Belieber! Usher has been a constant mentor and friend to JB ever since he first saw him sing in Atlanta. Himself a global superstar, Usher knows the entertainment business inside out and he's always ready with support and advice whenever Justin calls.

PATTIE MALLETTE

Pattie is hands down, the most-important person in Justin's life. She's been with him every step of the way, encouraging him and supporting him at every stage of his life. Since Justin found fame, she's become a name in her own right. She has more than 1.5million Twitter followers and is the successful author of 'Nowhere But Up'.

"Because Justin's on tour so much, we have to be creative to spend time with each other. But we're just like any mother and son. I am so proud of him!"

JAZMYN BIEBER

Justin's lil' sister Jazzy is given the ultimate VIP treatment any and every time she hangs out with her big brother! The little cutie has appeared on stage with Justin at many shows and has always gets a hugely warm reception on TV talk shows.

JAXON BIEBER

JB's baby brother is another Bieber with a fan club! When Jax was just one, JB sent hearts swooning around the world when he tweeted a picture of him holding Jaxon inside his jacket! These days, whenever he can, Justin spends time with his baby bro and often invites him along to red carpet events.

BRUCE AND DIANE DALE

With Pattie working so many hours to make ends meet while Justin was a young kid in Stratford, his grandparents Bruce and Diane played a major role in his upbringing. Wherever he is in the world, Justin stays in close contact and he rushes back to Canada whenever he can, to spend time with them.

RYAN BUTLER AND CHAZ SOMERS

JB met his best mates Ryan and Chaz at school and even though their lives have gone in totally different directions, they frequently hang out together. "I'm really proud that he put himself out there and was found, out of millions of people," proud Ryan has admitted. "Still, I miss him and feel sad he hasn't been able to play sports like other kids and do the usual kid stuff."

MAMA JAN

Jan Smith, better known as Mama Jan, is Justin's long time vocal coach. Over the years, she's worked with scores of big names in the music business and is widely considered to be the best in the world at her craft. Since hitting the big time, JB voice has recorded three full albums and done three huge world tours, all with Mama Jan by his side.

Take a quick look at JB's timeline on Twitter and you'll see just how important to him his fans are. He's constantly following fans and proclaiming his love and devotion to you. In fact, Justin calls his fans 'a family', what higher compliment can there be?

1. Justin was born in Stratford in Canada.

Just right ☐

Just bull ☐

2. The first time Justin's family realised he was musical was when he was just four-years-old.

Just right ☐

Just bull ☐

3. At Justin's school, the main language spoken was English.

Just right ☐

Just bull ☐

4. JB's best friends in Stratford were Ryan Summers and Chaz Butler.

Just right ☐

Just bull ☐

JUST RIGHT OR JUST

5. Growing up, Jeremy Bieber taught his son how to play lots of show tunes from musicals.

Just right ☐

Just bull ☐

6. Justin's first public appearance as a singer was busking outside the local theatre.

Just right ☐

Just bull ☐

7. Pattie posted video's of JB on YouTube; the first was Justin singing Ne-Yo's track 'So Sick'.

Just right ☐

Just bull ☐

8. Justin made his first trip to Atlanta to meet Scooter Braun in 2005.

Just right ☐

Just bull ☐

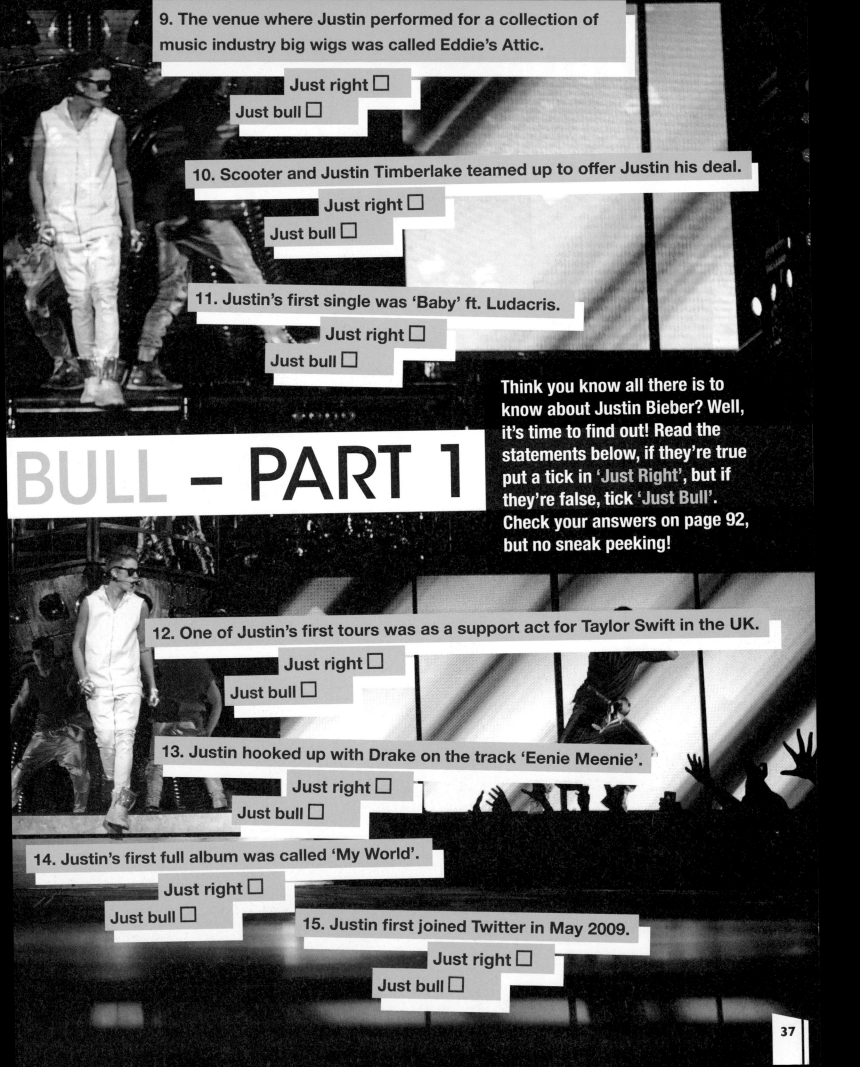

9. The venue where Justin performed for a collection of music industry big wigs was called Eddie's Attic.

Just right ☐

Just bull ☐

10. Scooter and Justin Timberlake teamed up to offer Justin his deal.

Just right ☐

Just bull ☐

11. Justin's first single was 'Baby' ft. Ludacris.

Just right ☐

Just bull ☐

BULL – PART 1

Think you know all there is to know about Justin Bieber? Well, it's time to find out! Read the statements below, if they're true put a tick in 'Just Right', but if they're false, tick 'Just Bull'. Check your answers on page 92, but no sneak peeking!

12. One of Justin's first tours was as a support act for Taylor Swift in the UK.

Just right ☐

Just bull ☐

13. Justin hooked up with Drake on the track 'Eenie Meenie'.

Just right ☐

Just bull ☐

14. Justin's first full album was called 'My World'.

Just right ☐

Just bull ☐

15. Justin first joined Twitter in May 2009.

Just right ☐

Just bull ☐

Sing WHILE YOU'RE Winning

2013

Virgin Media Music Award	Best Album (Believe)
Virgin Media Music Award	Best Solo Artist
Nickelodeon Kid's Choice Award	Favourite Male Singer

2012

American Music Award	Artist of the Year
American Music Award	Pop/Rock Male Artist
American Music Award	Pop/Rock Album (Believe)
MTV Europe Music Award	Best Male
MTV Europe Music Award	Best Pop Act
MTV Europe Music Award	Best World Stage Performance
Billboard Music Award	Top Social Artist
Nickelodeon Kid's Choice Award	Favourite Male Singer
MuchMusic Video Awards	Canadian Video of the Year (Boyfriend)
Juno Award	Fan Choice Award

1. WHICH ROYAL HONOUR WAS JUSTIN PRESENTED WITH, IN 2012?

2. JUSTIN WAS NOMINATED IN A MASSIVE SIX CATEGORIES AT THE 2013 WORLD MUSIC AWARDS, BUT WHICH OF HIS VIDEOS WAS UP FOR 'WORLD'S BEST VIDEO'?

3. WHICH SPORTING AWARD DID JUSTIN WIN IN 2011?

2011

American Music Award	Artist of the Year
American Music Award	Pop/Rock Male Artist
American Music Award	T-Mobile Breakthrough Artist
American Music Award	Pop/Rock Album (My World 2.0)
MTV Europe Music Award	Best Male
MTV Europe Music Award	Best Push Act
Young Hollywood Award	Newcomer of the Year
Teen Choice Award	Choice Music: Male Artist
Teen Choice Award	Choice Music: Breakout Artist - Male
Teen Choice Award	Choice Summer Music Star - Male
Teen Choice Award	Choice Music: Pop Album (My World 2.0)
MTV Video Music Award	Best New Artist (Baby)
MuchMusic Video Awards	Canadian Video of the Year (Baby)
MuchMusic Video Awards	UR Fave: Canadian Video (Baby)
MuchMusic Video Awards	UR Fave: New Artist
Juno Award	Pop album of the Year (My World)
Juno Award	New Artist of the Year

4. HOW MANY TIMES HAS JUSTIN BEEN NOMINATED FOR A PRESTIGIOUS GRAMMY AWARD?

2010

Brit Award	International Breakthrough Act
Billboard Music Award	Top New Artist
Billboard Music Award	Top Streaming Artist
Billboard Music Award	Top Digital Media Artist
MTV Europe Music Award	Best Male
MTV Europe Music Award	Best Pop Artist
CMT Country Music Award	Collaborative Video of the Year (That Should be Me)
Virgin Media Music Award	Best Solo Male
MTV Movie Award	Best Jaw Dropping Moment (Never Say Never)
MTV Video Music Award	Best Male Video (U Smile)
Nickelodeon Kid's Choice Award	Favourite Male Singer
Nickelodeon Kid's Choice Award	Favourite Song (Baby)
MuchMusic Video Awards	Canadian Video of the Year (Somebody to Love)
MuchMusic Video Awards	UR Fave Artist
Juno Award	Fan Choice Award
Juno Award	Pop Album of the Year (My World 2.0)

5. WHICH OF THESE AWARDS HAS JUSTIN NOT WON? CHOICE TWIT BEST HAIR WORST ALBUM HOTTEST MALE BEST CELEBRITY FRAGRANCE

Do You SPEAK Beli

In case you hadn't noticed, Justin Bieber is such a huge deal that being a fan requires mastering an entirely new language. Here are some of the key terms every Belieber should know.

Belieber
An obsessive fan of Justin Bieber.

Bieber Bullied
To be given a hard time by non-Beliebers.

Bieber Fever
Physical effect Justin Bieber has on female fans. Typified by symptoms including increased heart rate and feelings of faintness. See also Bieberculosis.

Leggo!
Meaning 'Let's Go!' Phrase frequently used by Justin.

Bieberculosis
Disease born of severe Justin Bieber love-sickness.

Überbelieber
Accolade awarded to the most obsessive of obsessive Bieber fans.

Biebergasm
Noun to describe sensation of excitement a fan might feel at seeing Justin Bieber.
E.g. "I was having a complete Biebergasm when he ran on stage!"

Bieberfied
To give a touch of Bieber identity to a person or object, by adding Bieber-related pictures, graffiti or memorabilia to it.
E.g. "I have Bieberfied my pencil case."

Biebergasted
To be stunned by the wondrousness of Justin Bieber or by things relating to Justin Bieber. E.g. "I was Biebergasted by Justin's Teen Vogue photo-shoot."

What would Bieber do?
Question to ask oneself when faced with a difficult situation.

eb'er?

Biebette
Name for a female überfan of Justin. See also Belieber.

Bieber Blast
To conspire with other fans to download a Bieber release en masse, in order to ensure it flies up the iTunes chart. E.g. "Let's Bieber Blast 'Believe' to number one!"

Bieberlicious
Word a Justin fan might use for something which is as hot or tasty as the man himself. E.g. "That guy is totally Bieberlicious."

Bieberstruck
Adjective used to describe a passionate or overwhelming feeling of love towards Justin Bieber.

Biebertastic
Word to describe something incredible, related to Justin Bieber.

O.M.B.
Acronym for 'Oh My Bieber' based on O.M.G. and used by excited fans. E.g. "O.M.B. Justin's new album is out on Monday!"

Shawty
Term favoured by Justin, to describe an attractive girl.

Eager Bieber
Term for a fan who will stop at nothing to meet Justin. E.g. "She's such an Eager Bieber, she camped outside the book signing for three nights."

Non-Belieber
Detractor of Justin Bieber, person or group to be avoided, also described as a Bieber Hater.

Holy Bieber!
Exclamation often used by Bieber fans. E.g. "Holy Bieber, I just won a meet and greet with Justin!"

Swag
An abbreviation of the word 'swagger', used in urban terms to describe style, coolness and confidence.

O.J.B.D.
Accronym for Obsessive Justin Bieber Disorder, a condition suffered by many fans. E.g. "Sarah is suffering from O.J.B.D."

Team Bieber
Part of the inner core. Only a loyal fan can claim membership to Team Bieber.

JUSTIN'S WORLD SEARCH

Globetrotting Biebz has been everywhere that's anywhere. Can you locate the destinations his Believe World Tour visited, in the grid below?

1. BERLIN
2. BIRMINGHAM
3. CAPE TOWN
4. CHICAGO
5. COPENHAGEN
6. DUBAI
7. DUBLIN
8. FRANKFURT
9. LONDON
10. MADRID
11. MIAMI
12. MOSCOW
13. OTTAWA
14. PARIS
15. SHANGHAI
16. VANCOUVER
17. VIENNA
18. ZURICH

P	A	R	I	N	E	R	E	V	U	O	C	N	A	V
N	W	O	T	E	P	A	C	I	I	Z	H	M	A	D
R	A	B	R	M	S	B	E	E	M	R	I	D	B	G
S	S	V	U	I	P	E	L	N	A	I	C	U	I	Z
N	A	T	F	M	L	R	R	N	I	C	A	B	R	U
I	E	B	K	A	O	L	M	A	M	H	G	A	L	R
D	V	G	N	I	N	I	P	A	T	O	O	I	I	I
N	A	S	A	L	D	T	H	R	D	R	S	N	N	C
I	N	E	R	H	O	G	C	H	I	R	S	C	G	H
L	C	N	F	S	N	O	T	T	W	A	I	R	O	T
B	P	I	B	I	M	E	S	H	A	G	A	D	L	W
U	A	L	M	N	O	V	P	R	I	S	M	O	S	O
D	R	R	Z	A	C	T	T	O	T	T	A	W	A	B
R	I	E	E	H	O	S	H	A	C	A	N	N	I	V
B	S	B	C	S	H	A	N	G	H	A	I	A	H	G

FEBRUARY 2013

Biebz sold quite a few copies at his the launch of his new book 'Just Getting Started' at WHSmith in London.

DECEMBER 2012

Awww! We always knew Biebz would be great with kids. Here he is with L.A. Clippers player Chris Paul's son, watching the Clippers play the Boston Celtics.

SEPTEMBER 2012

September 2012. JB popped up as the highlight on hit US shows Dancing with the Stars and America's Got Talent.

JULY 2012

In July 2012 there was news of a new love interest! Biebz snuggled with British internet sensations Sophia Grace and Rosie at the Teen Choice Awards.

JUNE 2012

Always about the fans; Justin posed for photos as he arrived for the Late Show with David Letterman.

PERFECT
P.A.'S

JUSTIN'S BEEN SO BUSY TOURING, IT'S AMAZING HE CAN BE BOTHERED TO GET OUT OF BED THE REST OF THE TIME. LUCKILY HE'S GOT ENERGY AND STAMINA BY THE BUCKETFUL. HERE'S WHAT HE'S BEEN UP TO IN THE WAY OF PUBLIC APPEARANCES.

NOVEMBER 2012

November 2012 saw Biebz surrounded by lovelies at the Victoria's Secret Lingerie Show.

MAY 2012

JB loves boxing and found time to watch the Cotto v. Mayweather Jr. fight.

MAY 2012

On the water in Norway.

MARCH 2012

Posing at Madame Tussauds in Berlin! Actually it was just his waxwork figure getting an update!

APRIL 2012

Justin hung with his homies Quincy Jones Brown and Alfredo Flores on Quincy's 'Stay Awhile' video shoot.

Karma Chameleon

Justin's early 'preppy' look has been replaced by a more mature, urban style

Hair Today…

Always a talking point, Justin's locks have come a long way since his trademark Bieber swoosh. Since then he's sported a shorter tousled crop, a slicked quiff, and his latest, undercut style.

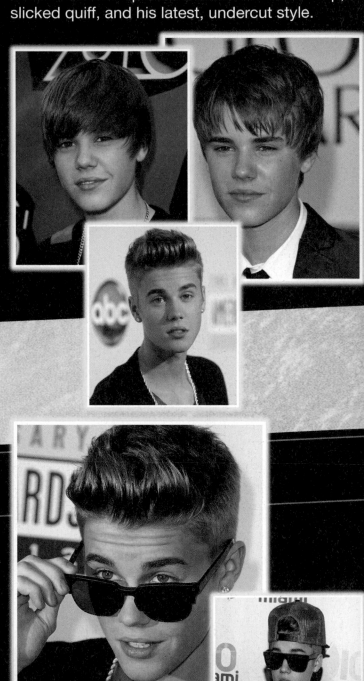

The Baseball Caps

JB has always loved baseball hats but they've got bigger and bolder in the past year. He's wearing them backwards, forwards and as high as possible.

The Shades

JB's rocking the eyewear this year. He looks great in frames of any shape or size – it's just such a shame to cover those gorgeous eyes!

The Beanies

Justin's also wearing his beanies with increasing ghetto swagga – including this bright red one.

The Bling

It don't mean a thing if it ain't got some bling. Justin loves jewellery and chooses his pieces with care. Watches, necklaces, bracelets and chains are all staples in his wardrobe.

STYLE & SWAG

Over the past year, Justin's personal style has evolved to match the shift in his music. The casual preppy separates of his early days have been replaced with fashion choices which are far more 'street'. Check out his latest looks.

The Brights

Biebz works vibrant pops of colour to the max, against a palette of neutrals or darks.

The Bold Statements

Whether it's a pair of scarlet slip-on, studded loafers worn on the red carpet, a casually slung bandana, pop-art prints or dare we say it, a gas mask, Justin is becoming increasingly confident with his style choices. He's willing to take a risk, make a statement and wear

All White On The Night

Where Justin's My World Tour was characterised by the colour purple, Believe is all about the colour white. White signifies rebirth and purity so it's perfect at this stage of Justin's career, underlining the fact that beneath all the hype, he's simply an artist and musician. Überstylists Kemal and Karla Harris were the visionary duo behind Justin's tour wardrobe, which showcased his maturing physique and perfectly partnered his new sound.

TAILOR MADE

Smart tailoring and natural materials kept JB crisp and cool during his high-octane dance routines.

PARACHUTE PANTS

Justin's fave low-crotched strides, gave him a deconstructed look.

SANS SLEEVES

With guns like that, no wonder sleeves are sooo last tour! Justin looked hunky in vests and sleeveless hoodies.

THE LEATHER LOOK

Not everyone can carry off head to toe leather – but JB can!

METALLIC TOUCHES

The palette of white was offset beautifully by artful touches of metallics, from gold gloves to silver wings. Justin simply shone on stage.

My Swag

Use these pages to make a moodboard to show your own totally swag style. Stick in photos, swatches of material and cuttings showing what you're currently wearing. Then make a wish list for you and JB for next season.

No one tweets like Biebz! Chances are you're one of his 36.5million (and rising!) Twitter followers, but have you been paying attention to his messages? Can you fill in the missing words of these classic JB tweets?

1. Wow. Airport was crazy getting to London! All worth it for my Beliebers. Some people always tryna ruin it for the fans. Not _ _ _ _ _ _ _ _ _ _ _ _ .

2. Eating _ _ _ _ _ _ _ and gonna get a good night's rest and relax. I hear u guys outside the hotel...and I LOVE U!

3. This girl sat on _ _ _ _ _ _ _ _ _ _ _ _ _ _ _ today in London. She was like "He isn't going anywhere."

4. Chillin with @ _ _ _ _ _ _ _ _ _ _ _ _ _ in the UK. Swaggy.

5. Being on promo feels really good. Glad to be back working and seeing the fans. _ _ _ _ _ _ _ _ _ _ _ _ . My fans go HARD!

6. Actually happy to be back out doing promo. Missed seeing everyone. Good day of interviews today. Just want # _ _ _ _ _ _ _ to get here already.

7. Who am I? The _ _ _ _ _ _ _ _ guy _ _ the _ _ _ _ _ _ . I'm a fighter for what I believe in but I have millions next to me. Thank you. #BestFansEVER.

8. It's funny when I read things about myself that are just not true. Why would certain people take time out of their day to _ _ _ _ on _ _ _ - year - _ _ _ ?

JUSTIN'S STORY III:

THE PERFORMER

A local talent show called Stratford Star was the scene of Justin Bieber's first public performance. The first prize was a shiny microphone, but for a 12-year-old Justin Bieber, the prize was of no importance; he simply wanted to find out if all the hours he'd spent practising at home would translate into a live show and whether he could connect with a real audience.

It took Justin just three songs to get his answer. JB sang Matchbox 20's 3AM, Alicia Keys' Fallin' and Aretha Franklin's classic Respect and came a very respectable third in the competition. Pattie, bursting with pride, recorded JB's performances and posted them on YouTube. The videos became the first of many but no-one could have predicted their success. People loved them. Each time Justin learnt a new song, Pattie would record it and put it online and as his talent grew, so did his internet fan-base.

Always looking for ways to improve, Justin knew that he needed more experience of singing live. There was a just one, small problem; the majority of normal performance venues aspiring musicians choose, such as bars and clubs, were strictly off limits to someone so young.

Justin quickly found the solution; he decided to take his talent to the streets! Every weekend, he'd strap a guitar on his back and head into town to sit on the steps of the Stratford Theatre and sing for passers-by. With his busking proving a hit with the people of Stratford and his YouTube videos garnering hundreds of thousands of hits, it wasn't long before the music industry started paying attention to the little kid with the big voice ...

As long as you love me [3x]

We're under [____],
[_____], billion [_____], in the world trying to [_____] in,
Keep it [_____],
[_____] on your face even though your [_____] is [_____],
But hey now, you know, girl,
We both know it's a [_____] world,
But I will take my [_____].

As long as you love me
We could be [_____], we could be [_____], we could be [_____],
As long as you love me,
I'll be your [_____], I'll be your [_____], I'll be your [_____],
As long as you lo-lo-lo-lo-lo-lo-lo-lo-lo-lo-lo-lo-lo-lo-lo-love me (love me),
As long as you lo-lo-lo-lo-lo-lo-lo-lo-lo-lo-lo-lo-lo-lo-lo-love me (love me).

I'll be your [_____],
Fighting every [_____] of the day for your [_____] girl,
I'll be your Hova,
You could be my [_____] [_____], on the scene girl,
So don't [_____], don't cry, we don't need no [_____] to fly,
Just [_____] my hand.

As long as you love me,
We could be [_____], we could be [_____], we could be [_____],
As long as you love me,
I'll be your [_____], I'll be your [_____], I'll be your [_____],
As long as you lo-lo-lo-lo-lo-lo-lo-lo-lo-lo-lo-lo-lo-lo-lo-love me (love me),
As long as you lo-lo-lo-lo-lo-lo-lo-lo-lo-lo-lo-lo-lo-lo-lo-love me (love me).

[Big Sean]
Yo, B-I-G
I don't know if this makes [_____], but you're my [_____],
Give me a time and place, and I'll [_____] and I'll fly you to it,
I'll beat you there,
Girl you know I got you,
Us trust...
A couple of things I can't [_____] without 'U',
Now we are on top of the [_____] 'cause that's just how we do ..
Used to tell me, "Sky's the limit", now the sky's our point of view,
Man now we [_____] [_____] like, "Whoa",
[_____] point and shoot,
Ask me what's my best side; I stand back and point at [_____],
You, you the one that I [_____] with, I feel like I need a new girl to be bothered with,
But the grass ain't always [_____] on the other side,
It's green where you [_____] it,
So I know we got [_____] baby true, true, true,
But I'd rather [_____] on this with you,
Than to go ahead and [_____] with someone new,
As long as you love me.

MISSING LYRICS:

As Long AS YOU Love Me

Next Stop LONDON

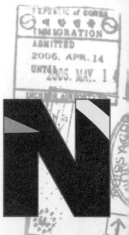

Loving It Live

Fans in the UK, across 10 dates and five cities, got their first taste of Justin's Believe Tour! Needless to say they weren't disappointed, as JB threw his all into every incredible show!

Birthday Partay

During his time in London, Justin turned 19 and used his time in town to celebrate his birthday in some of the city's top hot spots! He hit the LBC nightclub with celebrity pal will.i.am, dined at top notch restaurant Mint Leaf , partied at the Roadhouse in Covent Garden and the Project Nightclub and sent gossips' tongues wagging around the world when he enjoyed a birthday meal at the Lebanese restaurant Shashawi with Ella-Paige Roberts Clarke!

Dodgy Disguise?

After popping into the ultra-cool shop Acne for some retail therapy and relaxation, Justin made the headlines across the world again by attempting to evade the photographers' waiting lenses by wearing a gas-mask as a disguise. #Quirky!

JB's UK Base

While in town, Justin stayed in London's super-swanky Langham Hotel. Justin chatted to fans, who were a constant presence outside, every time he came in or out and often tweeted from inside.

Tour Craziness

Justin's UK jaunt certainly wasn't without incident! Paparazzi pressure on him was intense and during the London leg of the tour at the O2, JB made the headlines around the world when technical glitches caused the show to run late. "Because of some technical issues I got on at 10:10pm so I was 40 mins late to stage," he tweeted. "There is no excuse for that and I apologise for anyone we upset. However it was a great show and I'm proud of that."

The following night he was early on stage, but after playing his set, he suffered from breathing difficulties and was taken to hospital. Fortunately he was quickly given the all clear and the tour went on!

Fan Friendly

JB was never alone during his stay in the UK, his unbelievable fans accompanied him everywhere!

Not So Mellow Yellow

When JB makes a fashion statement, everyone knows about it! When he paired a spiky yellow baseball cap with pink trousers for a day out, it was trending on Twitter in minutes. Beibz later revealed his garish look was actually a dare! "Ryan Butler said 'you won't go out in that.' Justin later admitted. "I said 'watch me!' haha! It was maybe too colourful, next time I'm gonna wear a black hat. But a fan did get me this so I'm glad I wore it!"

Literary Lad

Somehow, between the tour dates, parties and paparazzi, Justin also found the time to launch his book, 'Just Getting Started'.

Makin

BELIEVE CHARITY DRIVE

When Justin released his Christmas album, 'Under The Mistletoe', he also launched his charity appeal. JB revealed he would be donating a portion of his earnings from the record to the seven charities closest to his heart. "I am launching the Believe Charity Drive because I know first hand that if you believe in your dreams, everything is possible," he said. To date he has raised $1,192,004!

www.justinbiebermusic.com/ believecharity

MAKE-A-WISH FOUNDATION

The Make-A-Wish Foundation aims to make dreams come true for seriously ill children. Many of them wish to meet their Justin and the empathetic star is only too happy to oblige. Justin invited four Make-A-Wish children to star in the video for 'Pray' with him and out of the spotlight he has spent his free time visiting children in hospitals and hospices around the world.

www.wish.org

g A DIFFERENCE

JB is passionate about using his position to help people. Whether it's by sending a supportive tweet to a fan, recording a charity single, or raising millions for causes close to his heart, Justin loves to help and urges and inspires his fans to do the same. Justin supports many charities, here are just a few causes close to his heart.

PENCILS OF PROMISE

Justin's manager, Scooter Braun has a brother called Adam, who has set up his own charity and JB's a big supporter. Pencils Of Promise aims to make a basic education available to everyone, no matter what part of the world you're from.

www.pencilsofpromise.org

IT GETS BETTER PROJECT

The It Gets Better Project was set up for young gay, lesbian, bi-sexual and transgender people dealing with their sexuality. Going through your teenage years can be tough if you feel different to everyone else. Justin has made videos, sent many tweets and talked about the issue on chat shows to let people know there is hope.

www.itgetsbetter.org

CRISIS PREGNANCY CENTRES

When she was still a teenager herself and pregnant with Justin, Pattie lived in a pregnancy centre. While there, she was given parenting lessons and support, and she and Justin have always been grateful for the help she received. In 2012, Pattie helped produce a short film, 'Crescendo', in a bid to raise money for the centres.

Creative Cover Art

Single

Does Justin's CD cover art always set your pulse racing? What would you like to see on the front of his next release? Get creative and design artwork for your favourite album and single on these pages. Then why not snap your work and tweet it to the star.

Album

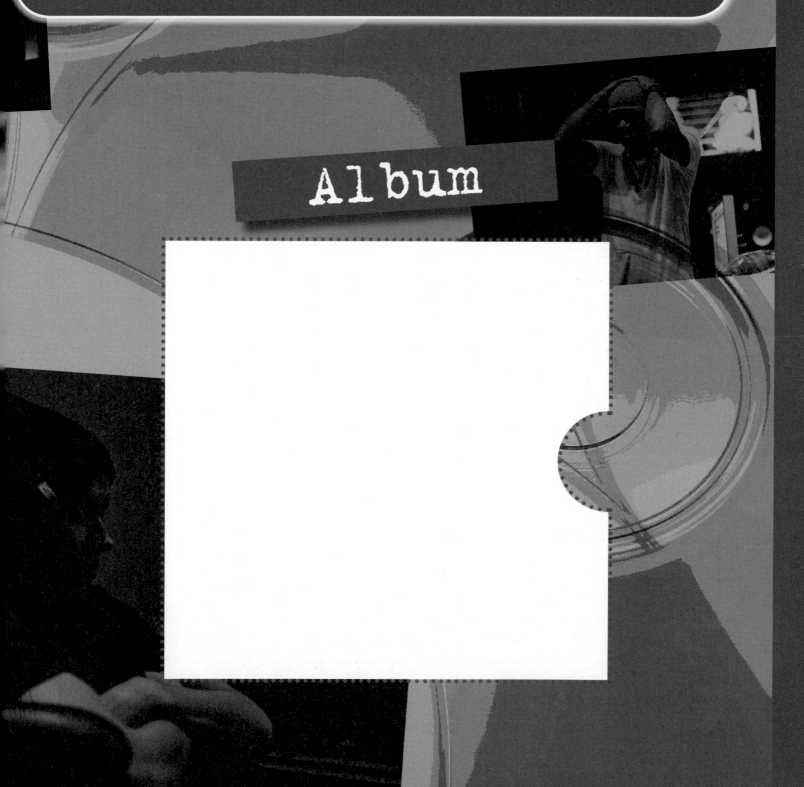

LUSTIN' FOR JUSTIN:
Big Day Out

If you spend every night dreaming of meeting Justin, here's where you set down those thoughts.
Use these pages to imagine a meeting with the man himself. You could draw up an itinerary of things you'd do – maybe you'd go skateboarding, have a jam session or go for pizza with friends.
Write down the things you'd talk about too.

LUSTIN' FOR JUSTIN:

Snap Happy

How would you and JB look together? Here's how you find out. You'll need some photos of yourself – if you don't have any you want to cut up, then you could colour-copy them first. Now grab a pile of pix of Biebz from magazines or on-line articles. Have fun cutting and matching backgrounds to create realistic looking 'couple snaps' and then compile a photo album complete with captions like 'Me and Biebz on the beach' or 'Out on the town.'

LUSTIN' FOR JUSTIN:
Belieber zone

Room overflowing with cuttings from magazines, ticket stubs and general Bieber-phernalia? Keep all your memories safe with a cool Belieber collage. Grab a glue stick or some sticky tape and get arty with a shrine to JB.

Cute, Single,  & Free to Mingle

Justin's currently enjoying being young, free and single, but he's not the kind of guy who shies away from a serious relationship. He wrote 'Boyfriend' about what he could offer the right girl. Use the next page to describe why you'd be his perfect partner. You could even pen a song about it.

BOYFRIEND

If I was your boyfriend, I'd never let you go,
I could take you places you ain't never been before,
Baby, take a chance or you'll never ever know,
I got money in my hands that I'd really like to blow,
Swag, swag, swag, on you.
Chillin' by the fire while we eatin' fondue,
I don't know about me but I know about you,
So say hello to falsetto in three, two, swag.

I'd like to be everything you want,
Hey girl, let me talk to you.

If I was your boyfriend, never let you go,
Keep you on my arm girl, you'd never be alone,
I can be a gentleman, anything you want,
If I was your boyfriend, I'd never let you go, I'd never let you go.

JUSTIN'S STORY IV:

BIG BREAK

"Justin is truly talented. He is that special superstar that you see once in a lifetime," Scooter explains. *"He plays four instruments, self-taught. He showed that in his YouTube channel. He had an incredible tone in his voice. He was captivating."*

If you were a big name star and wanted to organise a party in Atlanta in 2007, there was only one person you could call to get the job done! Scooter Braun was known as the finest party planner and promoter in the city. All the big acts would call on him to set up a party when they passed through. But, just like Justin, Scooter was always looking for ways to improve. Despite his reputation in Atlanta, Scooter wanted more. And in the summer of 2007, he found it.

One day when he was sitting at home, browsing videos on YouTube, Scooter stumbled across a video of a young kid belting out R&B songs. He knew immediately this boy was special and that if he could get Justin in contact with some of the big names he'd been working with in Atlanta, it could spell big things for both of their careers.

"When I met him, his personality won me over," Usher revealed. *"When he sang, I realised we were dealing with the real thing."*

It took some work, but Scooter eventually managed to get a message through to Pattie. For a while, she wouldn't take his calls but eventually she called back (Pattie says she rang simply to tell him to stop calling her). The pair had a two-hour conversation. They talked about many things; Justin's talent, the videos, Atlanta and more and Scooter asked Pattie to give him a chance to show them he was genuine. Pattie eventually agreed to a meeting in Atlanta.

In Atlanta, Scooter backed up every promise he'd made. He introduced JB to Usher and world-renowned vocal coach Mama Jan, and set up an industry showcase at a venue called Eddie's Attic, filling the room with some of the music industry's most important people..

Usher, quickly fell under Justin's spell that night and decided there and then to set up a company with Scooter and offer Justin a record deal.

JB's time had come ...

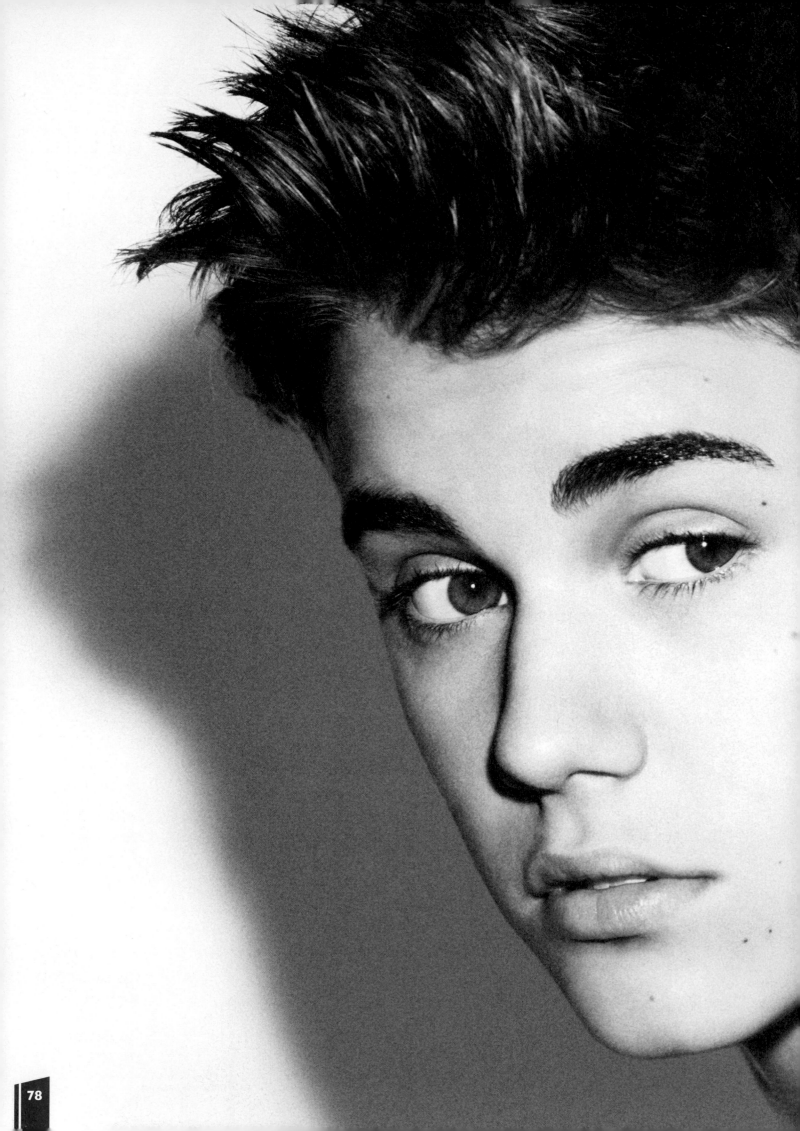

JUSTIN BIEBBER

Survival Expert
Bear Grylls

American rapper
Lil' Wayne

Swedish Electro Pop Artist
Karin Park

U.S. Screen Star
Zooey Deschanel

Football Legend
David Beckham

Reality TV Star
Spencer Matthews

First Lady of the United States of America
Michelle Obama

Hollywood Hard Man
Michael Madsen

Former World Heavyweight Boxing Champion
David Hayes

EVERYONE KN

Justin's life is so crazy that his connections spread far and wide.
Can you work out how the surprising spectrum of people below, have been linked to the star? Match each person with the statement connecting them to Justin

Was accidentally splashed with green gunge while JB was being gunked at an awards show.

Victim of a cyber-attack like Justin.

Seen partying with Justin in London.

Beats Justin up in one of his music videos.

Has sparred with Justin in the gym.

Has made the cover of Forbes Magazine due to his wealth, just like this person.

This person's family reportedly sells Justin Bieber goods through their company.

Her Royal Highness The Duchess of Cambridge
Kate Middleton

Pro-golfer
Bubba Watson

Business Magnate
Sir Richard Branson

Ever heard of six degrees of Kevin Bacon?

It's based on the theory that anyone in the showbiz world can be linked to Kevin Bacon in six steps or less. Can you figure out how it can be done with JB? We've started you off ...

Justin Bieber appeared in the 2010 TV musical film 'School Gyrls' with actor Greg Brown ...

OWS

Have become unlikely BFFs and talk and text every day.

Interested in playing in Justin's celebrity soccer side.

Shares a fashion stylist with JB.

Covered one of Justin's recent hits.

Lets JB skateboard on the ramps on his roof.

1. Justin is one of the most followed stars on Twitter, in fact he adds a new follower every five seconds.

Just right ☐

Just bull ☐

2. JB took to Facebook in 2012 to reveal that 'Boyfriend' would be the first single off Believe.

Just right ☐

Just bull ☐

3. Justin hooked up with hit singer/songwriter Mike Posner to record the track 'Boyfriend'.

Just right ☐

Just bull ☐

4. JB hit the road with the Believe Tour in September 2012. The first date was in Portugal.

Just right ☐

Just bull ☐

JUST RIGHT OR JUST

5. JB and his crew hired out an aircraft hangar in 2012 to rehearse for his world tour.

Just right ☐

Just bull ☐

6. Carly Rae Jepson was Justin's main support act on the American leg of the Believe Tour.

Just right ☐

Just bull ☐

7. In total, Justin clocks up an amazing 124 shows on his latest world tour.

Just right ☐

Just bull ☐

8. In 'Beauty And A Beat', Justin sings that he wants to party 'like it's the year 3000'.

Just right ☐

Just bull ☐

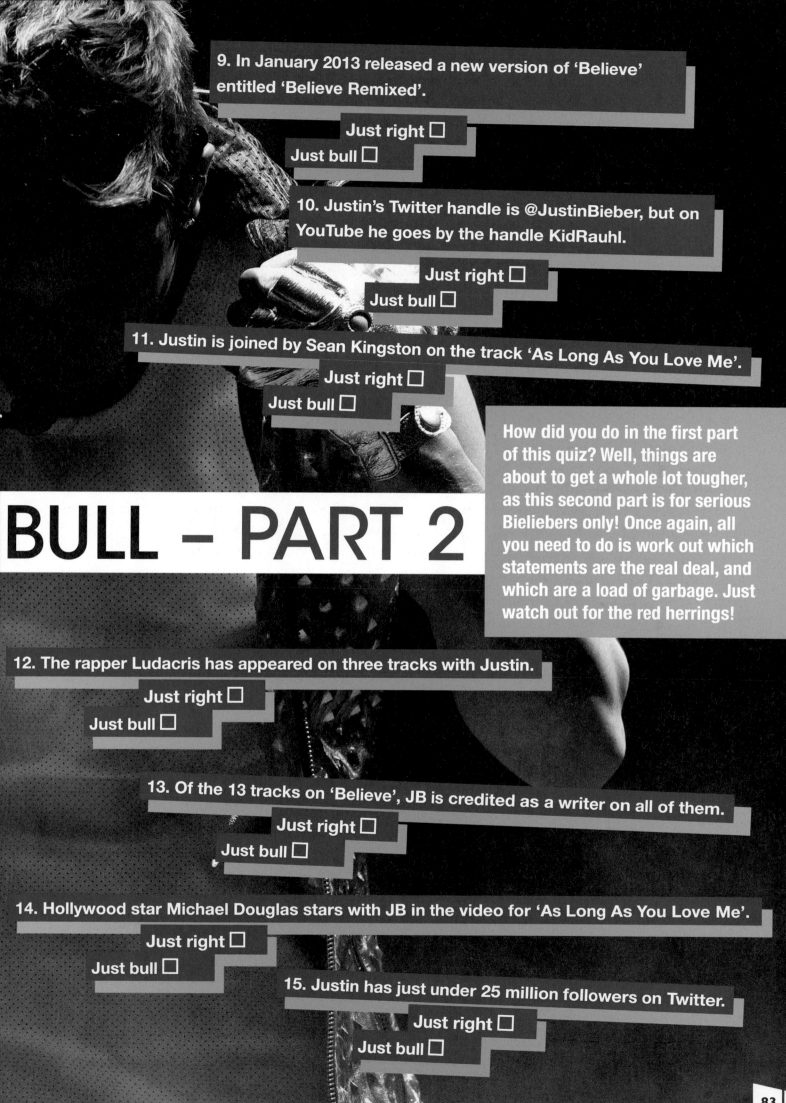

9. In January 2013 released a new version of 'Believe' entitled 'Believe Remixed'.

Just right ☐
Just bull ☐

10. Justin's Twitter handle is @JustinBieber, but on YouTube he goes by the handle KidRauhl.

Just right ☐
Just bull ☐

11. Justin is joined by Sean Kingston on the track 'As Long As You Love Me'.

Just right ☐
Just bull ☐

BULL – PART 2

How did you do in the first part of this quiz? Well, things are about to get a whole lot tougher, as this second part is for serious Bieliebers only! Once again, all you need to do is work out which statements are the real deal, and which are a load of garbage. Just watch out for the red herrings!

12. The rapper Ludacris has appeared on three tracks with Justin.

Just right ☐
Just bull ☐

13. Of the 13 tracks on 'Believe', JB is credited as a writer on all of them.

Just right ☐
Just bull ☐

14. Hollywood star Michael Douglas stars with JB in the video for 'As Long As You Love Me'.

Just right ☐
Just bull ☐

15. Justin has just under 25 million followers on Twitter.

Just right ☐
Just bull ☐

Fooling around with pal Quincy Jones Brown on the set of his 'Stay Awhile' music video shoot.

Proving he's game for a laugh, Biebz appeared on comedy show Saturday Night Live with Bill Hader and Fred Armisen, playing characters including a dork and a sk8ter.

HAVIN'

Biebz and mentor Usher always have a good time, especially at award shows like the Billboards.

Even stars as big as JB get slimed at Nickelodeon's annual Kids' Choice Awards!

FUN

HE MAY TAKE HIS MUSIC SERIOUSLY BUT JUSTIN ALWAYS HAS TIME FOR FUN. CHECK OUT THIS GALLERY OF GIGGLESOME SHOTS.

Justin and pal Lil Twist love performing together. Here they are at Club Nokia.

Good sport Justin cracked up when hostess Jenny McCarthy pounced on him for a kiss at the American Music Awards.

VIDEO CLIP CROSSWORD

ACROSS

3. This insanely cool clip was shot at Raging Waters Theme Park in San Dimas. (6,3,1,4)
4. JB and Jaden were shown messing around in the studio in the clip for this track (5,3,5)
6. Video filmed in a bowling alley in Universal City Walk (4)
7. Justin and Boyz II Men were shot on the steps of a classic Brown Stone building (2,2,2)
9. Studio-based vid, with JB 'tutting' with Usher (8,2,4)
10. Video shot on location in the Atlantis Paradise Resort in the Bahamas (5,3,3,2)
11. Model Rachel Barnes was getting up close as Justin's girlfriend in this video (9)
12. Macy's department store in New York was closed for this all-night video shoot with Mariah Carey (3,1,4,3,8)

DOWN

1. As part of the 'Arthur Christmas' soundtrack this clip featured Biebz in Santa's workshop (5,5,2,6,2,4)
2. Biebz and pal Sean Kingston were shot at a house party for this track (5,6)
5. Justin was seen petting some puppies in the clip for this song (3,4,6,4)
8. In this video JB gets roughed up by a famous Hollywood Tough Guy (2,4,2,3,4,2)

Solve the clues about Justin's incredible music videos then complete the crossword with the names of his tracks.

JUSTIN'S STORY V

THE NEXT LEVEL

Once Justin signed with Scooter and Usher, he stepped into a whirlwind. He was plucked from his day-to-day existence in Stratford and almost immediately was living the life he'd always dreamed of. He was recording an album with the best in the business, his YouTube videos were clocking up insane numbers of views and Usher was giving him a celebrity apprenticeship to die for.

In early 2009, JB released 'One Time', the debut single from his E.P. 'My World'. It hit the charts not just in his native Canada, but around the world and won him a legion of new fans, every one of them eager to hear more about this cute singer with the killer voice.

Nobody had seen an artist like JB before. Not only did he have the voice, he could play instruments, dance like crazy and look great doing it! Respected artists were queuing up to work with him, yet despite all his success, fans could still interact with him directly on social media. It was a unique and winning phenomenon.

After releasing several singles and an EP in 2009, Justin finally dropped his first album in 2010 and headed out on the road. JB wasn't just famous; he'd become a superstar! But could he keep the run of success going? Only time would tell ...

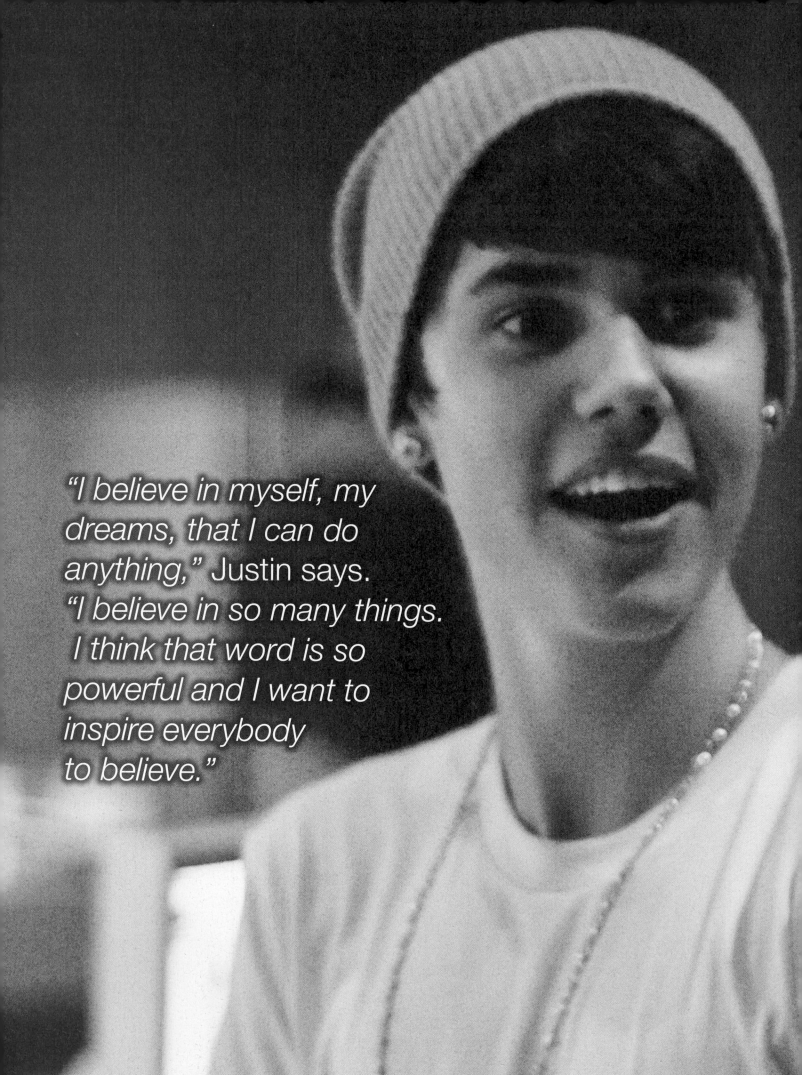

"I believe in myself, my dreams, that I can do anything," Justin says. "I believe in so many things. I think that word is so powerful and I want to inspire everybody to believe."

JUSTIN'S STORY VI:

TODAY, TOMORROW, FOREVER

Three smash hit albums, countless hit singles, record-breaking world tours, appearances on hit TV shows across the globe, acting gigs, a hit movie, millions of Twitter followers, billions of YouTube views later – Justin Bieber has achieved global success on an unimaginable scale.

The combination of his natural talent, winning personality and an unbelievable work ethic have allowed him to reach such heady heights and stay there. Incredibly he refuses to rest on his enviable laurels, continuing to strive and develop. His image, style and music have matured and his loyal fans have grown with him. The music industry is littered with once-great artists who tried to change their style only to find out too late that the fans didn't want this. Not so with Justin. Each step on his musical journey has surprised and delighted his Beliebers who continue to support and adore him.

"I believe in myself, my dreams, that I can do anything," Justin says. *"I believe in so many things. I think that word is so powerful and I want to inspire everybody to believe."*

We believe JB, we believe!

Answers

PAGES 26 – 27
MISSING LYRICS: BEAUTY AND A BEAT

Young Money,
You off, you off
Billion
Party
Finer, life
Forget, young
Need
Make, life
You
Music, move
Like
Body rock, body rock
Bow, ticket
Party
Show, finer
Forget, young
Need
Make, life
You
Music, move
Like
Ink
Tour, letters,
Justin Bieber
Selena
East, priest
Streets

PAGE 36
JUST RIGHT OR JUST BULL – PART 1

1. Just bull. Justin was actually born in London, Ontario, Canada.
2. Just right. Pattie knew he had something special when he started picking out songs on the piano, guitar and drums.
3. Just bull. Justin went to a French speaking school.
4. Just right. Justin, Chaz and Ryan were inseparable.
5. Just bull. Jeremy Bieber used to play rock tracks to his son.
6. Just bull. JB first performance was at a local talent show.
7. Just right. Justin's version has become a YouTube classic.
8. Just bull. Two years too early. JB headed to Atlanta for the first time in 2007.
9. Just right. Usher and a whole host of music execs packed into Eddie's Attic to hear JB sing.
10. Just bull. Although Timberlake did show interest, Scooter and Usher signed JB up.
11. Just bull. 'One Time' was Justin's first release.
12. Just right. The pair hit the road together in 2010.
13. Just bull. JB recorded 'Eenie Meenie' with his friend Sean Kingston.
14. Just bull. Trick question! Justin's first album was actually called 'My World 2.0'. My World was an E.P.
15. Just right. JB's first tweet asked fans to check out his first single, 'One Time'.

PAGES 38 – 39
SING WHILE YOU'RE WINNING

1. In 2012 he was presented with the Queen Elizabeth II Diamond Jubilee Medal. This is a commemorative medal to mark the 60th anniversary of the accession to the throne of Queen Elizabeth II.
2. 'Beauty and a Beat' was up for Best Video.
3. Most Valued Player at the NBA All-Star Celebrity Game.
4. He's been twice nominated for a Grammy Award.
5. Justin has never won 'Best Hair'.

PAGES 42 – 43
JUSTIN'S WORLD SEARCH

PAGE 52
TOP TWEETS

1. Today swaggy
2. A steak
3. The hood of my car
4. @JeremyBieber
5. We still got it
6. #BELIEVE
7. The luckiest guy on the planet
8. Hate on a 16-year-old

PAGES 58 – 59
MISSING LYRICS: AS LONG AS YOU LOVE ME

Pressure

Seven, people, fit

Together

Smile, hart, frowning

Cruel

Chances

Starving, homeless, broke

Platinum, silver, gold

Soldier

Second, dreams

Destiny's Child

Stress, wings

Take

Homeless, starving,

broke

Platinum, silver, gold

Sense, hallelujah

Rendezvous

Spell

World

Stepping out

Cameras

You

Argue

Greener

Water

Issues

Work

Start

PAGE 82 - 83
JUST RIGHT OR JUST BULL – PART 2

1. Just bull. Incredibly JB notches up a new follower every two seconds.
2. Just bull. It was Twitter.
3. Just right.
4. Just bull. The first date of the Believe Tour was actually in Glendale, Arizona.
5. Just bull. The Long Beach Arena in California was the scene of the Believe Tour rehearsals.
6. Just right.
7. Just right.
8. Just bull. JB's actually hoping to party like 'it's 3012'
9. Just bull. The album was actually called Believe Acoustic.
10. Just right. Justin took the name from his dad who goes by the screen name Lordrauhl.
11. Just bull. Rapper Big Sean features on the track.
12. Just bull. Ludacris appears on Baby and All Around The World.
13. Just right. JB had a major hand in every track.
14. Just bull. Michael Madsen co-stars.
15. Just bull. More than 36million of us follow JB on Twitter!

PAGES 80 – 81 EVERYONE KNOWS JB

David Hayes has sparred with Justin in the gym.

Michelle Obama got hit with some collateral gunge, when JB was getting slimed at the 2012 Kids' Choice Awards.

Lil' Wayne lets JB skateboard on the ramps on his roof.

Zooey Deschanel and Justin have both been styled by powerful styling duo Kemal and Karla.

Swedish Electro Pop Artist Karin Park covered Justin's track, 'As Long as You Love Me'.

Michael Madsen beat Justin up in the video for 'As Long as You Love Me'.

David Beckham has expressed interest in playing in JB's celeb soccer side.

Kate Middleton's parents reportedly sell Justin merchandise through their Party Pieces business.

Golfer Bubba and Justin have struck up an unlikely friendship and talk regularly.

Made in Chelsea star Spencer Matthews was photographed coming out of a party attended by Justin while in London.

Sir Richard Branson and Justin have both made the cover of Forbes Magazine

Bear Grylls was a victim of a cyber-attack, like Justin.

JB's Six Degrees of Kevin Bacon

Justin Bieber was in the 2010 TV musical film 'School Gyrls' with actor Greg Brown ... who appeared in the movie 'He's Just Not That Into You' with Jennifer Aniston ... who co-starred in the 1997 rom-com 'Picture Perfect' with Kevin Bacon!

PAGES 86 – 87 VIDEO CLIP CROSSWORD

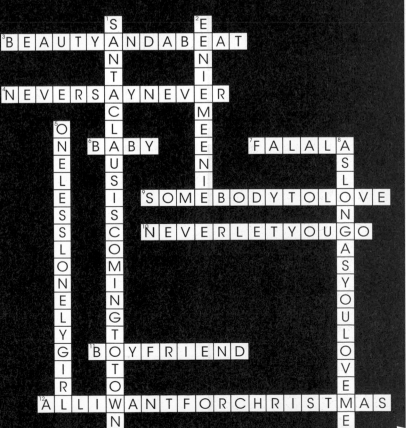